Safety Starts Here

Key Points to Developing a
Workplace Safety Program in Alberta

By: Stephen H. Johnson

Table of Contents

Introduction

Welcome to the Wonderful World of Workplace Safety.

My name is Stephen Johnson. I feel fortunate that I get to spend my workdays thinking about the workplace safety of others and myself. I am an Occupational Health & Safety Specialist.

I have not always been keen on safety. I can think back to jobs early in my working life when a disregard for safety that resulted in improved productivity was a method I routinely used to impress management. I viewed reporting a safety incident as a declaration of incompetency. I had a misguided belief that wearing safety boots protected me from any and all workplace hazards, and safety glasses were a forehead fashion statement. I even lent support for a union pushback against wearing electronic dust monitors at one job. I was the guy that thought management only tried to make workers wear personal protective equipment (PPE) as a way to control and ridicule workers, kind of like human dog collars.

My attitude toward safety changed for me

several years ago. I had always worked at companies that had safety incidents resulting in injuries. I assumed they were part of the working world. But this particular day was different. I was working at a large construction job site and we experienced a nightmare. The worst incident ever is a fatality. We tragically had a double fatality, with others injured. It was a different contractor involved, but I knew some the people, and some of the first responders. My life changed after that event. I was barely involved with workplace safety before this event, but I've spent almost every working day since deeply immersed in safety. I wish I could say it was the last time I around the loss of life at work, but it wasn't.

So better late than never, I discovered that I was pretty good at Occupational Health & Safety, both in education and in its practical application. I think it's due to my desire to actively share my knowledge with others and to know I'm working toward a truly necessary cause. I have made the business case to justify safety spending to executive level management, and I have conducted field orientation training for workers first day on the job. Effective safety management for me needs to reach and convince every single person in an organization.

This book has been written for smaller employers in Alberta who want to integrate safety into their business for all the right reasons. The right reasons being to protect life and property, to develop a strong business, and to ensure regulatory compliance.

If these reasons don't resemble your reasons to develop a safety program you may want to reevaluate your motivation to do so. This process is not easy or fast and it requires a continuous commitment to be successful.

This book is a starting point on your safety journey. It will get you thinking, acting and further researching your specific safety needs.

There is a lot more to workplace safety than any one book can possibly provide. This book is <u>not</u> intended to replace professional advice and it is <u>not</u> a guide to government regulations. Adherence to all laws and regulations is the sole responsibility of the reader. But, it will better prepare you to seek out resources and professionals.

Enjoy the journey; it's a continuous one.

Chapter 1

Seriously, Why Should I Bother?

Integrity is doing the right thing, even when no one is watching. C.S. Lewis

I can certainly understand your initial hesitation. After all this process is not easy cheap, or quick. It's difficult to find the resources and time necessary to complete a major project like this and you need to be sure there will be true value in your efforts. Time and money is needed to put a safety program together and time and money will also be required to maintain a Safety program. This is definitely not a "set it and forget it" kind of policy. Once all the work is been done to put a safety program together and someone will need to keep up the momentum to maintain the program long term.

After all, don't employees only care about their paycheck anyway?

Research has consistently shown that rate of pay does not even make it into the top three concerns for employees. Time and time again a secure workplace (which includes safety) has made it into the top concerns for workers in North America. Employees who feel secure will be more productive and remain on the job longer.

As part of your cost-benefit analysis you can add up the cost of not having a safety program.

I have presented many cost estimates on incidents to management personnel over the years. Never once have I heard someone say the cost estimates were lower than what they expected. The fact is All incidents even minor ones are grossly expensive. Some monetary cost for incidents continue long after they have been forgotten from memory. This can include WCB premium increases insurance rate increases legal cost and the cost of lost opportunities for the business.

Another thing to consider when deciding to form a safety program is your professional reputation.

So many things in a business are adversely affected by a poor safety record. You can lose potential customers if they don't want to be aligned with a company that is seen as a potential hazard. Industry peers will be hesitant on forming joint ventures with you. Your overhead cost will be higher. You'll likely have difficulty attracting and retaining employees. After all, when there's a choice why would you want to work somewhere that's potentially hazardous, or at a company that doesn't care about worker safety.

If you were under the impression that all press is good press, just ask a company if they feel the same way after a workplace injury. Sometimes four years later that impression will be all the public remembers once the media does an investigative story on the incident. There's no need to make yourself such a target.

In so many ways a poor safety record is also an invitation for lawsuits.

Because it's the right thing to do, Morally.

After an incident occurs everybody within an organization comes together united in a common goal. That goal is preventing the incident from ever happening again. A good safety program allows you to prevent the incident before it ever happens in the first place. It's like your own in-house insurance policy with a lot more benefits.

Employee turnover and the loss of experienced workers to other jobs erodes your employee morale. No one wants to work where there is little regard for personal safety. Your best employees have the most opportunities to go to other jobs and will take that opportunity if you don't care about them enough. The cost of employee turnover can be as staggering as employee injuries.

True industry leaders want to do everything they can to improve their business. A solid safety program is definitely in line with continuous business improvement.

Actually there's also a legal obligation, too.

The Occupational Health & Safety Act, Code and Regulations will outline the obligations all employers must ensure. So in reality you don't really have a choice whether or not to have safety program. Your choice is only in how good of a program you wish to put together.

Be careful in trying to put together a lean and discount safety program. Courts have an expectation that you will closely follow what's called "industry best practice" which is looking at similar businesses to yours and determining what most of them would have in place for similar circumstances. If your programs fall below this, a court could determine you did not provide adequate protection to have prevented an incident.

Beyond just the regulations covered under Occupational Health & Safety, there are many other regulations based on specific industries you will need to research and take into consideration all regulations that apply to your business. Things like the transportation of dangerous goods, specific motor carrier regulations, working alone legislation, just to name a few.

In the end you'll be glad you put together a complete and proper safety program.

It can be a very rewarding process to put together a safety program if you have the right attitude. If you don't have the right attitude, don't start. Strong management commitment is essential to success.

Don't worry, there's lots of help available if you know where to look. We'll cover that together later in this book.

Chapter 2

My Workforce isn't Motivated to Work Safely.

Monkey See, Monkey Do.

I'm paying them well enough; I expect safe work for that.

This is a complete misconception. There exists an innate lack of self-protection on the job. It's difficult to determine exactly why, in some cases it's because there is a worker perception that a workplace is safe because other people in the past have completed the same tasks (belief based on task history). However, all workers require (at a very minimum) proper instruction on the job, feedback, and safety training.

As discussed in the previous chapter, pay is not at the top of the list when it comes to employee motivation to work. Simply offering a decent pay rate has no connection to employees deciding to work safely on their own.

If you remain convinced that you can use pay to motivate safe work, consider implementing a safety incentive into your pay plan. That way you can accomplish proper communication to the workforce for your desire to have people take personal responsibility for safety. Incentives tied to safety have always had good intentions behind them. But, they have not escaped controversy either. The implementation plan to safety incentives is usually where the program flaws can be traced.

No one wants to develop a program that promotes unreported incidents just so a prize can be awarded. Many companies in recent years adopted the flawed model of rewarding large groups of people with a reward for remaining injury free for a predetermined length of time.

There are several issues with using the no-incidents reward model. The first thing to look at is if this simply drives out reporting incidents. Will it create an environment of potential hostility toward a worker who does suffer a workplace injury and thereby reduces or eliminates the incentives to the group? As safety professionals know, all incidents, near misses, and observations, are learning opportunities toward prevention. No one is interested in turning off the learning for management while simultaneously putting workers at risk, all under the guise of a promoting workplace safety.

In the United States, OSHA (the Occupational Safety & Health Administration) has looked into the potential negative impacts of some safety incentive programs. OSHA treats safety incentive programs that create a disincentive to reporting as unlawful retaliation under Section 11(c) of OSHA, and may sanction employers for implementing those programs.

The second thing to consider in a no-incident reward model is individual worker control toward the outcome. While safety is a group effort, it can be difficult to instill a sense of empowerment to an individual in this case. True buy-in comes from involvement. When someone is initially motivated to be part of a program, they need something specific to do. To be told "just don't get hurt for a year" is almost condescending. It also delivers a destructive (and false) message to employees that there is very little that individual workers can do to work toward injury reduction.

While there are more issues to consider in a no-incident reward model, a third and final one I will mention is the adverse reaction that occurs to employees when they do hear of an incident that eliminates or reduces the reward. Concern for the worker injured quickly fades, and may be replaced by feelings of helpless loss, disappointment, or even hostility toward those involved.

So, what can be done to accomplish the goal of effective and productive safety incentives?

Looking at the issues discovered in past incentive programs to give hints to the fine-tuning needed.

Keep incentive programs away from being tied to incidents or reporting. Ultimately, incidents are the result of a failure somewhere in a health and safety program for those of us who believe that all injuries are preventable. Penalizing all employees when an incident occurs isn't fair. After all, while safety is everyone's responsibility, they all weren't responsible for the incident. Instead, consider incentive programs that reinforce positive safety behavior.

The quickest impact may be a program that allows for some kind of instant recognition or reward. This allows the incentive program to gain momentum over time by constantly reinforcing workers actions. Rewards in this situation can be smaller value items like coffee gift cards to offer instant value. If the incentives are higher value items like jackets or electronics, the instant reward can be points given to the employee that can be banked over time toward the larger item. This type of reward system may also create an environment of positive competition amongst employees as more and more people try to match or exceed the success of their co-workers in obtaining rewards.

Incentive rewards are also a great means to reinforce safety learning. Safety meetings don't always hold the full attention of the participants. This is particularly true when covering low-occurrence, but still important safety topics.

Is it their fault, or yours?

The employees work for you, so what example are they following when it comes to safety?

Everything in a business flows from the top down, and attitudes about safety are no exception. If front line crew members are reluctant to listen to management, it may be a sign of a deeper issue. Why are they reluctant? Do they believe safety is just another plan to be pushed onto workers by management? Is it seen as a responsibility being downloaded on an already maxed out workforce?

All management need to "walk the walk" when it comes to safety. Otherwise it's hard for a workforce to believe that safety is a true company priority, especially over other priorities like productivity.

In order to eliminate a communication "broken telephone", make sure you develop a direct link to the front line. Hold meetings with everyone, not just posted memos or mandates given to supervisors. Employees need to feel like they are part of something bigger, and part of the process itself in order to offer true buy-in to a safety program. After all, a safety program is essentially for the workers anyway, they should have a change to be directly involved in the process, and the maintenance of their safety program.

Are the safety conscious workers seeking peer permission first?

Everyone wants to be safe at work. However, no one wants to be seen as a troublemaker or a boss' pet. This is particularly true in new employees who want to please many of their coworkers. This time for new employees is also when they develop their job habits, so it becomes a very important time to establish proper safety expectations.

If a new employee enters an environment where senior staff disregard the rules, take safety shortcuts, and think they are immune to injury, then this way of thinking and acting will become normal behaviour to new people who are seeking to fit in with their new work environment.

Your safety program needs to be applied to all employees. Existing and new workers, from management to the front line, everyone needs to be involved. When expectations are set from day one, and being followed by all people in an organization, good habits form quickly. Your safety program need to deliver the message that safe work isn't just ok, it is expected.

Hiring for experience brings someone's unknown bad habits to your workplace too.

Not many people talk for very long (if at all) about safety during a job interview. Although it is starting to penetrate the Human Resources world now.

Any new hire (or temporary worker) brings undisclosed shortcuts and safety attitudes into your workplace. When we hire someone, we're always optimistic that we've selected someone who will be a good fit for the company and who can adequately do the job. But it's harder to tell if they will do the job in exactly the way expect, safely that is. New worker orientations are not just for the no experience hires. Establish expectations though education with everyone who walks through your door to work.

Chapter 3

How much is this going to cost?

Resistance at all costs is the most senseless act there is. Friedrich Durrenmatt

I'm not going to insult your intelligence with double talk.

The response about cost of a safety program that I know will make you want to throw this book against the wall is "a lot cheaper than the cost of incidents". But seriously, that's not helpful.

I know you some real ways to measure the financial resources needed. As a responsible business, you need to budget properly for everything thing you do. It's important to plan for your safety spend.

Now for the good news.

You can afford a safety program! A bold statement considering I have no idea what your business is or your circumstances. But, knowing the fundamentals involved in developing a safety program I know you can put together a program even with no direct money to put toward the program. The money you would have spent will, however, be replaced by a significant increase in personal effort.

The positive effect of making your program on your own without outsourcing or spending much money is how intimate you will become with your content. You'll effortlessly know it inside out and backwards. There will be no question at all about your commitment to safety.

You have some choices when it comes to balancing the direct money you spend on program development. The easiest choice, but also the most expensive, is to outsource the complete safety program development to a consultant. Depending on the complexity of your business the price will vary, but no matter how complex or simple your business is, count on this method to be priced in the thousands of dollars. Because I know you want value for your spend, I will caution you to be hesitant to select any consultant to build an entire system at a discounted rate. You may be disappointed in the quality you receive.

The second and opposite method is to research and put a program together by yourself, or using only internal existing resources within your company. I say opposite method only because this way saves the maximum amount of upfront cash required. This method would be most ideal for very small businesses such as owner operators, or for start-ups with few people and lower risk tasks.

The method most recommended is a combination of both. Designate one internal person to coordinate the project, directly involve as many people as reasonably possible from all departments, and invite an outside consultant to advise and review through the process.

Don't forget the step of having all your final paperwork reviewed by an employment lawyer first before rolling it out to the staff. Fine-tuning for legal compliance is an important step. Should you ever need to appear in court to justify or defend your safety program, having it legally reviewed in the very beginning will make things so much easier for your defense. That being said, it's also a good idea to have the program reviewed after any major changes and additions. For minor changes that happen over time, you may wish to schedule a periodic legal review that looks at several changes at once rather than even tiny revision. Your legal counsel should be able to work out a revision plan that works for your business.

Chapter 4

Ok, Who Needs to Do What?

The way to get started is to quit talking and begin doing. Walt Disney

Start at the Top

A formal safety program is a serious an ongoing commitment. That commitment starts at the top with senior management.

When done properly, it holds accountability because it becomes so transparent, very visible, and an ingrained part of your corporate culture. A safety program isn't something that is just on file at the lawyer's office in case of trouble some done. It does not act as an insurance policy that allows you to transfer the risk of an incident to someone else.

A written statement of management commitment should be at the forefront of your safety program. It should be prominently displayed at your workplace for all to see. It should also be on your website. This is a good thing, promote it. But, it will also force accountability. You wouldn't want to publically commit to workplace safety, and then be questioned on your actions later.

A safety program, as mentioned previously, is a project without a true end date. So, it requires ongoing responsibilities balanced with accountabilities.

Management's biggest responsibility will be to provide the appropriate resources toward the safety program development and maintenance. Things like training budgets, safety specific staff meetings, safety administration costs, a means of communicating safety information (posters, wallet cards, hard hat stickers). It also falls to management to ensure the competency of all workers. No matter who is assigned the task of worker training and review, management must have a way to ensure this is happening properly.

Every employer must take every reasonable precaution to ensure the workplace is safe, train employees about any potential hazards and in how to safely use, handle, store and dispose of hazardous substances and how to handle emergencies, supply personal protective equipment and ensure workers know how to use the equipment safely and properly, and to immediately report all critical injuries to the government department responsible for OH&S, appoint a competent supervisor who sets the standards for performance, and who ensures safe working conditions are always observed.

Front Line Supervisors are going to be very important to upholding your safety program. These are the people with the greatest direct influence on the way things are done. One of the best ways to establish safety accountability is to measure safety performance as a part of Supervisors regular performance reviews. When something gets measured, reported and reviewed, then it tends to get done.

Supervisors must ensure that workers use prescribed protective equipment devices, and must advise workers of potential and actual hazards, and must take every reasonable precaution in the circumstances for the protection of workers.

Workers are not without their own specific responsibilities. All workers must have a responsibility to work in compliance with OH&S acts and regulations, a responsibility to use personal protective equipment and clothing as directed by the employer, a responsibility to report workplace hazards and dangers, and a responsibility to work in a manner as required by the employer and use the prescribed safety equipment.

In addition to workers having responsibilities, they also have specific rights when is comes to workplace safety. Employees have the right to refuse unsafe work, the right to participate in the workplace health and safety activities, the right to know, or the right to be informed about, actual and potential dangers in the workplace.

Dedicated Safety Person

The decision to establish a specific paid position within your company to handle Health & Safety matters will primarily be decided by the size of your organization. As we covered earlier, just by having an employee dedicated to safety does not allow you to transfer all responsibility for the program to this one person. The specific responsibilities for all people in the organization remain. The specific safety employee is often called a Safety Advisor because they are someone who provides advice and direction in relation to everyone's safety tasks. They act as an extremely valuable resource for the vast amount of safety administration that constantly needs to be done to uphold a safety program.

If your organization cannot justify the cost, or do not have enough work to justify the time of a full time person, check with safety consulting firms in your area who may be able to provide specific services to fill this gap until you grow into requiring a full time employee to care for your safety program.

Add-on responsibilities

You may also consider making a current employee with other responsibilities into the person who also has internal safety administrative responsibilities. But be sure these additional tasks do not overwhelm the person to the point that things do not get done in a timely and accurate manner. You will also need to ensure sufficient and on going safety training for the individual. Most importantly, the person needs to really want to do these tasks. Don't forget about adding a layer of accountability. Someone needs to make sure everything is still being completed. Consider this method of safety administration a temporary fix that should be periodically reviewed. Safety rarely remains a part-time function.

Chapter 5

What is this COR thing and why do I need it?

Some people don't like change, but you need to embrace change if the alternative is disaster. Elon Musk

A brief explanation of COR

COR stands for Certificate of Recognition. It is a part of an incentive program designed to encourage businesses to implement health and safety systems that meet certain specified standards. Occupational Health and Safety department of the Province, along with the Workers' Compensation Board administer the programs.

The belief behind the program is that cooperation between government and business does more to reduce the human and financial costs of workplace injury and illness than a regulatory approach can accomplish.

The program offers discounts on WCB premiums to companies upholding a standardized safety program, and proving so though internal and external audits.

For smaller employers, there is a certificate called SECOR. This stands for Small Employer Certificate of Recognition. It covers employers with less than 10 total employees. Once you cross that threshold into your 11th person, you must then get a regular COR.

A Certifying Partner will help you set up a health and safety management system and get a COR.

There are 13 Certifying Partners authorized to administer the Certificate of Recognition (COR) program to Alberta employers. Chapter 8 (Where Do I Turn For Help?) has a list with corresponding industries to help you select the best Certifying Partner for your business.

For some companies, based on their industry rating for WCB premiums, the discounts can be substantial and in some cases can fund their entire annual safety related expenses.

COR goes beyond just being a discount program. In recent years, industry has been using it as a pre-qualifier for work. Many prime contractors in the construction and oil industry will insist on bidders being COR compliant to work on their sites.

COR can also be used as a marketing tool. It's a major accomplishment that should be celebrated. Many companies proudly promote their COR on all sales literature, letterhead, website, and advertising. It shows an ongoing commitment to safety.

Starting Steps

To obtain a COR, you will need to align yourself with a certifying partner. These are industry specific safety associations who will also provide the audit protocol for you to follow. A list of certifying partners in Alberta appears in this Chapter 8 of this book.

Then you need to build or modify your safety program to meet or exceed the standards set out by the certifying partner. When building or modifying your safety program, keep in mind you're not just looking to meet a pre-set criteria. You want your program to provide the best quality for your employees. This is the reason why many companies end up exceeding the standards in some sections, to keep worker safety as the priority.

Audit Survival

What a terrible word to use, audit. Is there anyone besides auditors who like this word? It brings up thoughts of government revenue agents picking apart every last detail and happily assigning penalties.

But a COR audit is different. In some years, you are completing your own internal audit. It's a great opportunity to make sure your program is working correctly and it gives you the chance to correct any deficiencies or make corrections.

Every third year, you will require an external audit. These can be a little more tense for companies, but they don't have to be. An auditor who does not work for you, comes in to your business and reviews documentation, observes work being performed, and interviews a selection of employees from senior management down to the front line workers. The auditor's job is simply to measure the safety program against the criteria laid out in the audit. It is not for the auditor to make personal judgments. It is a snapshot in time using a selection of data. All auditors are different, but the audit results should be the same. They should be closely following the protocol.

The best part about an audit is that it doesn't come as a surprise. This is a scheduled event, and you know all the questions in advance. So, the best way to get ready for an audit is to test, test, test. Think of it as an open book exam. Run through mini audits on your own well in advance of the external auditor's arrival to prepare.

If you don't have time to do it right, how will you find the time to do it twice? If you fail a section of the audit, you will have some limited time to correct the issue and then have what is called a Limited Scope Audit. Under this type of audit, another external auditor comes in to perform an audit only on the section that did not pass the first time. Save yourself the trouble by over preparing for your first audit. After all, a failing grade means there is a weakness in your safety program and that could lead to an incident. Prevention should be the whole purpose of your program.

Chapter 6

Defining the Culture You Want

A nation's culture resides in the hearts and in the soul of its people. Mahatma Gandhi

Where you were, where you are, and where you're going.

A culture in any organization will not change quickly or easily. It runs a lot deeper than developing a good program, and it goes beyond the words you speak. It can be summed up as the "personality" of your company.

A safety culture is formed from the safety beliefs shared by the majority of the workforce. If safety was not regarded highly before developing your safety program, and you met with a lot of resistance while implementing it, expect a lot of time and effort before your safety culture begins to shift.

Your culture is a combination of normal practices, assumptions, policies, stories, prior experiences, priorities, responsibilities, accountabilities, and even values and myths.

Your safety culture, like your safety program, needs to start at the top. Senior management needs to truly believe in taking care of the safety needs of all employees. A culture doesn't improve by just having good intentions and forcing people to adapt.

A positive safety culture is built on three principles. Understanding, skill, and attitude. An understanding of how to do something, the experience to do it, and the desire to do it correctly. Management's job is to make sure these elements are sufficiently in place for all employees.

If you were to describe your ideal safety culture on paper, you want it to ultimately match up with the eventual behaviour of employees.

Steering your Safety Culture

To obtain buy-in to your safety vision, empower everyone. All employees have a part to play in active safety management.

Safety is not a spectator sport. The more actively involved people become, the more likely they will be to adopt a positive outlook on safety. Everything from reporting potential workplace hazards, correcting deficiencies, even the ability to intervene on unsafe work are all things that empower employees while strengthening the effectiveness of your safety program.

Remove blame from safety and focus on learning. Some workers believe that near miss situations and minor incidents are things that get employees in trouble. If they think this way, they're likely to cover up anything that goes wrong. Without the information on an incident, no correction can be investigated. Your near misses and minor incidents are your most powerful information sources to make improvements before something major happens.

At one place I worked, I shifted the worker attitude toward near misses. Instead of viewing them as a negative thing, I gave an incentive to the crew for finding and reporting any hazards they could find. I made it a little easier by also having employees report on positive safety observations. The data collected in the first month exceeded the entire previous year. It allowed for a massive amount of safety corrections and hazard elimination. Employees no longer felt the need to avoid reporting hazardous situations. It also produced a great feeling of ownership of the safety program amongst all employees. That became the most valuable part of this plan. It established trust and communication across all levels within the company.

To ensure a positive movement in your safety culture, safety needs to be integrated into everyone's job. As an agenda item in meetings, as a reporting section in management reports, and as a part of news releases and corporate updates.

Safety milestones and accomplishments should be celebrated and promoted. Winning safety awards, and setting a new record for continuous days without an incident are achievements that are a result of everyone's joint efforts.

Positively reinforcing desired behaviour is the quickest way to experience change. The effect of this will spread when employees begin to seek out this reinforcement because it feels good. This is the relationship they will develop with certain positive actions.

Measuring safety culture progress

There is no standard measurement to gauge a culture. Behavioral analysis will help you understand the general safety attitude of your workforce. If your safety statistics are showing an improving trend over time its likely due to an improving safety culture.

Watch for and address any early warning signs that you can identify. These issues do not get better or correct themselves in time. They amplify and spread. They also take a very long time to reverse because by the time a weakness can be measured in the safety culture, a failure somewhere in the program has already occurred.

When your safety culture begins shifting in the right direction, you're winning in a big picture way.

Chapter 7

Safety for Stronger Profitability

Safety brings first aid to the uninjured. F.S. Hughes

Making money from your safety program.

There's no doubt there are significant costs involved with having an incident. Medical costs, lost time of the injured person, lost time of witnesses, lost time to investigate, increase in WCB premiums, lost time for a stand down meeting to review the incident details and implement corrective actions, worker distraction costs, administrative costs, legal issues, product and equipment damage. This is not even a complete list. In fact, for some companies the indirect costs of an incident can be as high as 5 times that of their direct costs. In the tragic case of a worker fatality, most of my cost estimates regardless of the company size are well in excess of one million dollars.

Don't just think of preventing injuries only.

The majority of workplace incidents involve product and equipment damage only. Many peoples mind goes directly to human health and life when they thing of safety, but its important to solve all sides of the puzzle. Product and equipment incident costs add up quickly. If they are included in your safety program, you will have established a tracking and correction mechanism. This will mean your safety program acts as a damage cost control model.

A proper safety program and its positive results will open doors to new business growth. To be a supplier of products or services to many companies, part of the vendor selection process will include a safety component. Don't comply and you won't get the work, no matter your price.

As a competitive advantage.

Actively promoting safety will put you at a competitive advantage over those who remain quiet about it. At this point you've spent money, you made a major high level commitment, and you changed your company culture. That is a massive accomplishment, promote it!

All incident costs are paid from profit dollars. Consider your typical profit margin and make some quick calculation for yourself on how much money you need to earn to offset an incident of say $5000, $10,000 or $15,000.

Chapter 8

Where Do I Turn For Help?

We can't help everyone, but everyone can help someone. Ronald Reagan

Start at the beginning

I highly recommend involving a Safety Consultant in the beginning from the planning stage of your safety program development. Even if your budget is thin, a consultant be involved in a way that fits your spend amount. Spending a bit of money in the beginning working with someone who has the knowledge and experience of doing this kind of work, will allow you to save a significant amount of time by focusing your efforts in the right way, and on the right areas.

Keep in mind; it can be more costly to correct a mistake later than it is to get it right the first time.

Industry associations and referrals from people in your personal network can put you in touch with Safety Consultants who work in your industry and your area. My suggestion is to always try to meet with a consultant in person to make sure their personality and business style matches well to yours. You'll end up working very closely with this person and you need to be able to accept their advice easily.

Partnership in Injury Reduction

Your industry certifying partner association for obtaining COR.

A Certifying Partner will help you set up a health and safety management system and get a COR.

There are 13 Certifying Partners authorized to administer the Certificate of Recognition (COR) program to Alberta employers.

Choose a Certifying Partner that has the right fit for your company and industry.

When choosing a Certifying Partner, you should consider the following:
- Which Certifying Partner best fits your company and industry.
- Where they offer training and its

availability.
- Safety services offered.
- Cost of training and services.

List of Certifying Partners:

Alberta Association for Safety Partnerships
Serving: All industries

Alberta Construction Safety Association
Serving: All construction related
companies

Alberta Corporate Human Resources
Serving: Provincial government and
regulatory agencies

Alberta Food Processors Association
Serving: Bakeries, Meat Packers,
Breweries, Retail & Food Services

Alberta Forest Products Association
Serving: Forest Product Manufacturers and
their contractors, Logging, Trucking of
Logs, Timber Management

Alberta Hospitality Association
Serving: Hotels, Motels and Convention
Centres, Industrial Camps, Hospitality

Industry Employers

Alberta Motor Transport Association
Serving: General and Specialized Trucking,
Garbage Hauling

Alberta Municipal Health & Safety
Association
Serving: Cities, Towns, Villages, and
Counties

Alberta Safety Council
Serving: All Industries

Continuing Care Safety Association
Serving: Public and Private Long Term
Care Facilities

Enform
Serving: All Petroleum Related Companies
Manufacturers' Health & Safety Association
Serving: Manufacturing, Machine Shops,
and Metal Fabricators

Western Wood Truss Association of
Alberta
Serving: Wood Truss Fabrication, Home
Improvement Centres

The government as a resource.

Laws are all public accessible and thanks to the Internet, can be quickly found and referenced.

Take the time to read and understand the Occupational Health & Safety Act, Code, and Regulations. This document is well laid out to quickly find the information you require for your business. Once you read it, your also realize that having it (or access to it online) is actually a requirement. So, saying you couldn't find a copy is no excuse for not reading. In fact, that itself would be a violation.

While all the information in the Alberta OH&S manual is valuable and important to know, pay particular attention to the employer and employee obligations under the law.

Don't only read the Alberta OH&S Manual. Be sure to read all the legislation that applies to your workplace and extract the safety information to include in your own safety program.

Keep in mind that laws are constantly changing. Set periodic review dates to make sure something new doesn't pass without your knowledge. Ignorance is no excuse for the law.

Industry Associations.

If there are any industry associations connected with your business, they can be a valuable resource regarding safety too. Network with others to find out trends and other information to strengthen your safety program.

There may be safety newsletters and trade publications that cover safety topics specific to your business. Sign up for anything online that appears to be relevant. Let the information come to you. But remember to actually read them!

Hire a Professional.

A qualified Safety Consultant has specialized education in Occupation Health and Safety, and can bring insight from experience working with many other companies and industries.

Whether full-time, part-time, review or advice, a Health & Safety Consultant can act in a similar manner to many other business professionals you may invite into your organization for specialized tasks, much like a third party financial advisor or a lawyer. You can tailor the time required to you budget and specific needs.

Some consultants will even have the ability to assist you remotely (depending on your particular needs). I personally have completed many consulting assignments using a combination of customer visits when needed, and off-site communication by email, telephone and document requests.

I also offer my consulting customers the protection of a flat fee price structure. By quoting work required by a customer in a fixed cost quote, customers can accurately budget and know in advance exactly what they are getting for their money. I stay away from hourly pricing. Customers get nervous not knowing how many total hours will appear on the final invoice.

Guarantee? You're kidding, right?

The final thing to look for in a Health & Safety Consultant is a guarantee. Yes, guarantee. It's something you typically won't find in many professional services at all. But, if you seek out a guarantee, you may be surprised and certainly pleased when you discover a professional willing to place a guarantee on parts of their service offering to you. I offer a guarantee on every consultancy agreement that I enter. From researching other firms and speaking to many other Independent Health & Safety Consultants, I am the only Health & Safety Consultant I could find in Alberta who offers a guarantee every time, without a customer needing to ask first. I have even heard of some consultants telling customers that their professional designations would be cancelled if they offered a guarantee to customers. This simply is not the case. You are not asking for a guarantee on future results, or a guarantee to pass an audit. But a guarantee on what the consultant will do for you is a perfectly acceptable business practice. However so, very few consultants will offer any guarantee.

Do your research. Select a consultant that is right for you based on the value you'll receive (not just based on the price you'll pay), also based on the industry expertise you require, and based on a personality that aligns with your company culture.

Conclusion

Endings to be useful must be inconclusive. Samuel R. Delany

This is not so much the end of a book as it is the beginning of your journey. By now you should feel like you can take control of the project of building a formal safety program for your business.

We started by discussing your "why" which is a big motivator for getting anything done. Hopefully your "why" is big enough to see it through.

We covered the costs involved for budgeting purposes, and then into an overview of everyone's responsibility during the process for you to get your team together.

An explaining of COR and the process followed if that is your goal.

When your safety culture starts to move in your predetermined positive direction, it's a great "executive summary" way to know your safety program is doing what it's designed to do.

The case was also made to justify the money involved in a formal safety program by explaining the different moneymaking and money saving safety opportunities.

In the last chapter, I even showed you where to turn for help.

So, any excuses are over. It's time for further action. Your beginning in this process is behind you now, you've already begun.

Continuous action, no matter how small, will move you toward your goal. Reach out for help when you need it, but just don't stop.

This is the end of my involvement in your process for now. But reach out to me if you think I might be a good fit to assist you more. My contact email is mentioned in my bio on the back cover of this book, and you could always contact me through my LinkedIn profile.

Good Luck!